Everything I Know About the Rat Race I Learned From My Cat

Everything I Know About the Rat Race I Learned From My Cat

by Allia Zobel

Illustrations by Nicole Hollander

Andrews McMeel
Publishing

Kansas City

For information, write Andrews McMeel Publishing, 4520 Main Street, Kansas City, Missouri 64111.

www.andrewsmcmeel.com

99 00 01 02 03 KWF 10 9 8 7 6 5 4 3 2 1

Library of Congress Cataloging-in-Publication Data
Zobel, Allia.
Everything I know about the rat race I learned from my cat / by Allia Zobel ; illustrations by Nicole Hollander.
p. cm.
ISBN 0-8362-6842-3 (ppb)
1. Cats—Humor. 2. Work—Humor.
3. Business—Humor. I. Hollander, Nicole. II. Title.
PN6231.C23Z68 1999
818'.5402—dc21 98-20926
CIP

For God; my husband, Desmond Finbarr Nolan; my parents, Alvin and Lucille; and for the whiskered wonders themselves—the dark and handsome, savvy and spectacular Winston Stanley III ("the thoid") and the elegant, gentle, and loving Vanessa Darling—who've mastered the best way to deal with the rat race: sleep through it.

—ALLIA ZOBEL

Acknowledgments

For my agent, Rita Rosenkranz; my editor, Patty Rice; and booksellers everywhere, who've made my rat race a lot easier. Thanks you guys.

Introduction

When it comes to the rat race, there is no better teacher than that adorable, four-legged ball of fluff you share your life (and probably your bed) with: your cat. Though she doesn't have an MBA, refuses to dress for success, and doesn't give a lick about positively influencing the boss, she innately knows how to get what she wants (often without even asking).

Whether it's a corner office with a comfy couch to nap on, or a key to the executive wash room where she can groom herself in private, cats inevitably get the lion's share of perks across the board—in business, at home, and in life in general. They never lose favor with the boss or get passed over at bonus time. They are never threatened with downsizing or forced to take early retirement. Even in today's uncertain business climate, a cat's position is as secure as it gets.

So what's their secret? A combination of things, really: unswerving loyalty, unconditional commitment, a confident attitude, complete focus on goals, and a strong belief that they deserve everything. As I discovered from research with my own upwardly mobile cats—as well as from feline focus groups around the country—they also adhere to a certain Strategic Action Plan (SAP). It's a fairly simple set of commonsense rules, which I've listed on the following pages.

Will reading this book ensure you a first-place finish in the rat race? There's one way to find out. So what are you waiting for? Enjoy!

—Allia Zobel

Don’t jump in the boss’s lap unless he asks you.

If at first you don’t succeed,
take a nap and try again.

Keep away from cafeteria tuna,
especially if it's on a VP's plate.

Be indispensable.

It's okay to drink from the executive toilet,
as long as no one's watching.

Think before you pounce.

ALOOFNESS CAN WORK IN YOUR FAVOR.

A set of sharp claws comes in handy.

Network or no work.

Don't climb the corporate ladder
if it makes you dizzy.

Not everyone who strokes you is your friend.

It's bad office etiquette to rub your nose
on your manager's wife.

Never underestimate the power of eye contact.

Watch your tail.

Every meeting must have an agenda.

HUPCHOO! I HOPE I DON'T HAVE A COLD.

CARE FOR A TISSUE? I HAVE THEM MADE FOR ME... IN FRANCE.

LE BON TISSSUE.

DON'T SHED ON THE CLIENT.

Never play cat and mouse unless you're the cat.

Walk all over everyone—
but don't let them step on you.

It never hurts to brush up against your supervisor's leg at raise time.

Always wear a collar on interviews.

Miss Lewis, I Ate ALL the Flowers in my office. Can I have yours?
Why don't I just call the Florist, sir.
It's Better to eat the Flowers in your own office than the ones on the receptionist's Desk.

It's impolite to lick a coworker's face
in the elevator.

Dress tastefully on casual day,
even if no one else does.

Never wash your private parts in the middle of the conference room.

Don't sit on the water cooler.

If you have to pull out tufts of hair,
do it in the hall, not your office.

Be flexible.

Make friends with your boss's secretary.

Whine less, purr more.

SAVE AS MUCH TUNA AS YOU CAN FOR YOUR RETIREMENT.

It's inappropriate to sit down in the middle of a presentation and scratch your head with your foot.

Don't try to influence the boss by leaving dead birds on his laptop.

The less paraphernalia you have on your office walls, the more you'll get promoted.

Mark your territory.

No job is worth getting your whiskers out of whack.

Support your company's flavor-of-the-month management style—especially if it's fishy.

If your boss finds a hair ball in your office, blame the cleaning people.

Food left unattended in the conference room for more than two hours is fair game.

It's politically incorrect to tell your secretary he has a nice tail—even if he does.

Short-sleeved shirts and white pocket protectors are a fashion no-no, unless, of course, the CEO wears them.

Bring your attaché case to company outings when there's a shrimp bar.

Never, *ever*, forget National Secretary's Day.

Avoid provocative clothing—
unless you're up for a salary review.

MAKE FRIENDS IN HIGH PLACES.

Bragging on your annual self-evaluation
is de rigueur.

Never give a straight answer.

Keep yawning to a minimum
at sexual harassment sensitivity seminars.

Be wary of coworkers who
put you on the speakerphone.

STAY HOME IF YOU HAVE FLEAS.

It's inappropriate to bet a client you can shake treats from the office vending machine—unless, of course, he gives you good odds.

Learn to talk in sound bites.

No matter what your manager says,
a cubicle is never better than an office.

Be inventive when it comes to budgets.

Flattery will get you everywhere.

Don't stick your paws
in the lunchroom salad bar.

Stretch often.

It's okay to suck wool, if you do it discreetly.

Keep PHONE CALLS At the OFFice SHORt AND Sweet, UNLess they're personAL.

Never judge an applicant by the
size of his beeper.

You can never have too many office toys.

Work like a dog
when your manager's watching.

Don't get caught playing with your mouse
when the computers are down.

TAKE TIME TO STARE OUT THE WINDOW.

If you have to hiss and spit,
close the door to your office.

Don't eat goldfish from the office manager's
desk; they could be booby-trapped.

Management expects you to
participate in employee happenings such as
Take Our Daughters to Work Day.

Good grooming is essential to success.

Never bring rat heads to the office,
unless you have enough for everybody.

Use lots of buzzwords "going forward,"
so that, "at the end of the day,"
you can be more "impactful" and wind up
in a "win-win situation."

Call in sick if you're in heat.

Be hard to figure out.

wear power RED to important Meetings.

Flying in the cargo hold is for animals.
Insist on business class, or first class
if the client's paying.

It's impolite to rip snags in your
administrative assistant's stockings.

Spell-check everything.

Use the litter box before you go to a staff meeting.

this is really nice of you.

Oh, it's such a good cause.

You can never buy too many Girl Scout cookies from the CEO's daughters

It's customary to bring in a note from the vet if you're out for more than two weeks.

If you want to upwardly influence your manager, don't chew on his telephone cord.

Show support for your department's
after-work sports teams.

Never swish your tail and bare your fangs
unless the competition does it first.

It's not professional to relieve yourself on your exit interviewer's rug.

Always make your manager look good.

Don't let coworkers see you faxing hair ball remedies to your friends.

Resist the temptation to draw whiskers on an Employee of the Month poster.

LAY DUMB IF YOU'RE CAUGHT EATING SOMETHING
rom the OFFICE REFRIGERATOR THAT ISN'T YOURS.

Taking home condiments from the
office kitchen is tacky…
unless, of course, you're having a party.

Business cards say a lot about you.

Keep your ears cocked for news when you're at the company gym.

It's unprofessional to lie on your back in the lobby and swat ornaments on the company Christmas tree.

Ms. tyler
Your 10:00
is Here.

SALLY, I'M SKIPPING
OUT ON MY 10:00.
MEET ME AT THE
AVIARY. Sue

Be careful what you write in E-MAIL messages

Bigger bonuses go to those who wear and
carry items bearing the company logo.

If you notice a bug on the wall
in your boss's office, don't just stare.
Excuse yourself and go eat it.

It's a good idea to trim the hair growing out of your ears before an annual meeting.

Restroom toilet protectors make great lobster bibs.

Leave your personal problems at home.

Never nibble at the plants in a junior partner's office.

Don't cry over spilt milk.

It's better to nap with cats than to lie down with dogs.

Stay current on office gossip.

A good secretary is worth her weight in fresh—not previously frozen—crab legs.

If you feel the need to crawl up someone's curtains, wait until after regular business hours.

Cultivate headhunters.

Grab the lion's share.

AN ILLEGIBLE SIGNATURE MARKS YOU AS A LEADER.

Be careful about recycling “Secret Santa” gifts.

It’s okay to let your boss rub you under the chin, but draw the line when it comes to your belly.

Don’t forget to take your originals
from the copy machine.

Spend time on the Internet wisely.

Blow your own horn.

Beware of video surveillance cameras in the office supply room.

Don’t let the executive committee
catch you with catnip.

The perfect screen saver? A photo of the boss.

they special-ordered it...from tuscany.
really?
It's not the size of the desk that counts, but how comfortable the chair is.

Be judicious in your use of little yellow stickies.

Keep track of mileage.

The “Help Desk” can’t do anything for a broken nail.

Never bring your kittens into the office unless it’s an emergency.

Being seen with members of upper management in company newsletter photos is good for your career.

Make a good impression with your voice-mail message.

Hide under the desk if you hear the word "reorganization."

It's bad office etiquette to sit on top of a report your secretary's trying to type.

In a dog-eat-dog corporate environment, cultivate feline tendencies.

The receptionist needs to know if you're on another floor sitting in a bag.

Never ask a secretarial candidate if he's neutered.

Be nice to everyone. You never know who could wind up being your boss.

Don't be pressured by solicitations for gifts for fellow coworkers. One dead bird per collection envelope is plenty.